REMEMBERING
Diana

REMEMBERING
Diana

Photographs by the

Daily Mail

ATLANTIC WORLD

Contents

Introduction	5
1981	14
1982	24
1983	30
1984	34
1985	42
1986	50
1987	54
1988	62
1989	68
1990	78
1991	88
1992	100
1993	112
1994	118
1995	124
1996	130
1997	134

Introduction

In the summer of 1981, a young woman married a prince and changed our perception of the British Royal family forever. She was the epitome of an English rose, he was the heir to the throne. On July 29th 1981, watched by millions of people worldwide, Lady Diana Spencer walked down the aisle to marry Prince Charles in a spectacular ceremony at St Paul's Cathedral. As the Archbishop of Canterbury noted at the time, *'This is the stuff of which fairy tales are made'.*

Born on the July 1st 1961, the third of four children, Diana was part of a family very familiar with the traditions of Royalty. As the result of their friendship with George VI and Queen Elizabeth, her maternal grandparents, Lord and Lady Fermoy, were offered the lease of Park House, which passed to Diana's mother, Frances Roche, on their deaths. Her father, Viscount Althorp, was appointed equerry to Queen Elizabeth II.

Following her parents' divorce in 1969, her father was granted custody of the children, and at the age of eight, Diana became a boarder at Riddlesworth Hall, a prep school in Norfolk. During the school holidays, she spent many days indulging her love of swimming in the estate's pool, and became a talented swimmer. Her first contact with the immediate Royal Family came around this time when Prince Andrew and Prince Edward would often drop by to play in the pool.

In 1973, she followed her sisters to West Heath boarding school in Sevenoaks, Kent. It was here that her talent for communicating with people was first noticed: as an early volunteer at Darenth Park, a large hospital not far from the school, her teachers realised how easily her warmth, laughter and compassion immediately put patients at their ease.

On the death of her grandfather in 1975, her father assumed the title of Earl Spencer, and she became Lady Diana. The family immediately moved to the family seat at Althorp, and a year later her father married Raine, daughter of Barbara Cartland. It was on the Althorp estate in November 1977 that Diana first met Prince Charles. She was revising to retake her 'O' levels and he had accepted an invitation to a shoot. School friends recalled that Diana had always idolised him and took pains to ensure she was home that weekend!

After failing her retakes, she joined the Institut Alpin Videmanette, a finishing school in Switzerland, but left after a term. A variety of courses followed and eventually Diana moved into a flat in Earls Court, given to her by her parents as an 18th birthday present. She began to work three afternoons a week at a private kindergarten in Pimlico, and despite the fact she had no formal training, Diana was a great success there; her natural gift of communication with the children was quickly noticed and soon her hours were increased.

During 1980, Charles and Diana met again at various events; the relationship began to deepen when she was invited to watch him play polo at Cowdray Park and then to join the party on board *Britannia* for Cowes Week. This was followed in September by an invitation to Balmoral for the traditional Royal Family gathering, which gave the young couple an opportunity to spend a great deal of time together. It was during this holiday that the paparazzi first began to suspect a new romance, and on her return to London, Diana was immediately pursued by the media; photographers camped outside her flat and pictures appeared in the press on a daily basis.

In late November and December 1980, the Prince embarked on a tour of India and Nepal and when he returned, Diana joined the Royal Family at Sandringham for New Year. Amid frenzied media speculation, Charles returned from his traditional skiing trip to Klosters at the beginning of February. A few days later, on the 6th, he asked Diana to marry him; she accepted immediately.

Their engagement was not officially announced until more than two weeks later on February 24th 1981. To protect her from growing media intrusion, Diana was moved first to Clarence House, the home of the Queen Mother, and then to Buckingham Palace until the day of the wedding, where she was soon thrust into the official duties of public life. Charles was determined to marry at St Paul's Cathedral and so preparations for the wedding quickly began in earnest. Over the next four months, details of the arrangements were poured over and commented on by the press and public alike. The BBC planned to broadcast the event to 74 countries, reaching an audience of 750 million. This was indeed a right Royal wedding.

Wednesday, July 29th 1981 dawned a perfect summer's day. Hundreds of thousands of people camped out along the procession route, eager to catch a glimpse of Diana as she drove past in the Glass Coach, with her father, Earl Spencer at her side. Millions more around the world sat glued to their television sets as she made the three-and-a-half minute walk down the aisle of St. Paul's to meet Prince Charles, with her twenty-five foot train billowing behind her.

After the ceremony, the jubilant crowd cheered them back to Buckingham Palace, where Charles kissed Diana on the Palace's balcony; an image that was splashed across front pages of newspapers worldwide the following day. After the wedding breakfast they spent three quiet days at Broadlands, the home of Lord Mountbatten, before joining the Royal yacht Britannia, for a honeymoon cruise around the Mediterranean, accompanied by 277 sailors! Disembarking in Egypt, the newly-weds flew to Scotland to spend a month at Balmoral with other members of the Royal Family.

A short tour of Wales, their own principality, followed in October; it was during this official engagement that the press dubbed her 'Diana, *the Queen of Hearts*'. It was also noticed how pale she had been looking, and public and press speculation was confirmed on November 5th, when it was announced they were expecting their first child the following summer. As the birth approached, Diana continued to oversee the redecoration of Highgrove, their country home.She was determined to have their first baby at St Mary's Hospital in Paddington, a revolutionary approach in Royal terms, as babies had traditionally been born at home. Prince Charles planned to be present at the birth, and after a difficult sixteen-hour labour, Prince William was born on June 21st 1982.

Diana's second pregnancy was announced in February 1984 and Prince Harry arrived on September 15th. Both she and Charles were determined that the boys would have as 'normal' an upbringing as possible; nannies were hired, but they both spent as much time with the boys as possible; the young princes attended kindergartens rather than being educated at home before prep school; they also delayed sending William and Harry to boarding schools until they enrolled at Eton College in their teens.

After Harry's birth, Diana gradually resumed her royal duties. By now, not only was she fully established in her role as wife to the future king, but she had also gained an international reputation as a fashion icon.

Determined to support her husband, care for her sons and carry out her official duties, she nevertheless knew she wanted something more fulfilling and was determined to make a difference to people's lives. By 1987 the AIDS crisis was fully established around the world; those suffering from HIV and AIDS were stigmatised and many saw it as a self-inflicted disease. During the year, Diana visited the first AIDS clinic in England at the Middlesex Hospital and shook hands with a patient. Such was her appeal and influence, this seemingly small gesture had an immediate and overwhelming impact. The image was broadcast around the world and allowed the professionals working in the field to begin to dispel the myths and prejudices surrounding the disease.

Diana's obvious pleasure and enthusiasm for good causes were in great contrast to her unhappiness in her marriage. Towards the end of the 1980s and into the early 1990s, it was becoming obvious that her and Charles' relationship was beginning to founder. Photographs were published of the two of them looking clearly uncomfortable in each other's company and they were spending more and more time

apart. In March 1992, her misery and distress were compounded by the death of her father, Earl Spencer.

Media speculation continued to mount during the year, culminating on December 9th 1992 with an announcement in the House of Commons by Prime Minister John Major of their official separation. Diana was now to live permanently at Kensington Palace whilst Charles continued to live at Highgrove.

Initially, the role Diana would play was unclear. She was determined to continue her charity work and began to organise tours with charities such as the International Red Cross. She also spent as much time with William and Harry as she could, taking them to everyday places such as Thorpe Park and Disneyland.

On December 3rd 1993, after a very successful year, Diana announced that she would be stepping down from public life. She pleaded a need for 'time and space' after so many years in the public eye. She did indeed cut down on her public engagements for a time, but her charitable work began to increase again over time.

The divorce was finally made absolute on August 28th 1996. Diana received a lump-sum settlement and was stripped of the title 'Her Royal Highness'. She again decided to reduce her charity work, apart from six organisations including the National AIDS Trust and the English National Ballet. But very soon she had taken on a new cause - the anti-landmine campaigns. Through the Red Cross, a working visit was arranged for January 1997 to Angola, home to 12 million people and an estimated 15 million landmines. She famously walked through a half-cleared minefield and publicly detonated a mine that had been found, to highlight their devastating effect. Yet again, an iconic image of her was flashed around the world and within a matter of days the landmine crisis had been brought to the forefront in countries worldwide.

In the summer of 1997, Diana and her sons joined Mohamed Al Fayed and his son, Dodi, on their yacht in St Tropez. A relationship between Diana and Dodi quickly blossomed and they began to see much more of each other. On August 30th, the couple enjoyed a quiet, private dinner together at the Ritz Hotel in Paris. On leaving the hotel, their Mercedes was followed by the paparazzi and the car crashed in the Alma Tunnel under the River Seine. Dodi and

the driver, Henri Paul, died immediately, while Diana and her bodyguard, Trevor Rees-Jones, were rushed to intensive care. The Princess died in the early hours of Sunday August 31st 1997, a month after her thirty-sixth birthday. Information was relayed to the Royal Family through the night and Prince Charles faced up to the daunting task of waking and telling their two sons of her death. The news was immediately flashed all over the world and a stunned British public, woke to the intense media coverage on the Sunday morning.

In the week that followed, public reaction to Diana's death was unprecedented and took on a surreal quality. At St James's Palace, members of the public, who did not know her personally, queued for up to twelve hours to sign a Book of Condolence. Similarly, at Kensington Palace, people poured into the grounds to leave flowers and heartfelt messages, which soon formed a fragrant sea around the house.

On Saturday September 6th, close to a million people lined the streets of London to pay their last respects. William and Harry walked the mile-long route behind the coffin accompanied by their father, their uncle Earl Spencer and Prince Philip. As the funeral cortège left Kensington Palace, there was total silence along the route, punctuated only by the tenor bell at Westminster Abbey tolling every minute and the noise of the horses and the gun carriage on which her coffin lay. As the funeral bearers carried her into the Abbey, television cameras picked out a card on one of the wreaths on the coffin which simply said 'Mummy': it was a last tribute from Harry.

The congregation in the Abbey included guests from all walks of life: royalty and show business stars sat alongside representatives from her various charities. The carefully planned service included a moving tribute from Elton John who sang a re-written version of *Candle in the Wind*. Her brother, Earl Spencer, gave a strong, emotionally-charged eulogy before the hearse set off towards the family estate at Althorp where she was to be buried on an island in the middle of a lake.

Never has the death of someone provoked such a global and lasting reaction. She left a deep impression on those she met when she was alive and her legacy lives on. She used her status and influence to campaign on issues that needed the public's sympathy and support and was genuine in all the work she did for these causes. Through her charities she met and touched countless people's lives and did what she was determined to do: she 'made a difference'.

Her finest legacy is William and Harry: 'her beloved boys', who were fifteen and twelve when she died. Their close bond with their father and each other since her death is clear and unequivocal. Both have matured into young adults with strong beliefs and principles; her influence will always be there. She would be intensely proud of them and of the fact that William has embarked on a new chapter in his life with his marriage to Kate Middleton.

A romance begins

The media first realised a growing friendship was developing between Lady Diana Spencer and Prince Charles in the autumn of 1980. After she was invited to holiday with Prince Charles and the Royal Family at Balmoral, she returned to London to find photographers camped outside her flat and the kindergarten where she worked. Diana was no stranger to the royals, her first home having been Park House in the grounds of Sandringham House. Her maternal grandparents had been great friends of King George VI and the Queen Mother and childhood playmates included Prince Andrew and Prince Edward.

Below left: A young Diana at her mother's house near Itchenor in West Sussex. Her parents divorced in 1969 and her mother Frances married Peter Shand Kydd.

Above left: The press were waiting outside Diana's London flat in November 1980. Despite constant questions, she refused to comment on her relationship with Prince Charles.

Below: With her eldest sister Sarah, Diana leaves Princess Margaret's party at the Ritz, in London.

A London address

Images of Diana were captured every time she left her London flat. When she was eighteen, She became entitled to a legacy left by her great-grandmother and used it to purchase a flat at 60 Coleherne Court, at the junction of Old Brompton Road and Redcliffe Gardens. Close friends then rented rooms from her. She mixed with the wealthy young set that lived around Sloane Square, dubbed 'Sloane Rangers' by the media. Weekends were usually spent in the country and she went skiing every year. After a brief spell at finishing school in Switzerland, she pursued a variety of courses and jobs, but eventually found employment three afternoons a week in the Young England Kindergarten, at St. Saviour's Hall, Pimlico. Fees were £200 a term and the children were generally from very wealthy families. Diana was an instant success at the kindergarten, popular with staff, parents and children alike. Despite the absence of any formal training, she demonstrated a natural gift for communicating with children and was highly praised by the principal, Kay Seth-Smith.

Kindergarten days

As she supervised the children from the kindergarten playing in St. George's Square, the famous shot was taken of 'Shy Di' wearing a Liberty skirt that became transparent in the sunshine. Apparently, Prince Charles on seeing the photograph remarked, 'I knew your legs were good but I didn't realise they were that spectacular. And did you really have to show them to everybody?'

Nanny Diana

After working at the kindergarten for a time, she also took
on the position as nanny to American businesswoman
Mary Robertson, looking after her son Patrick for two
afternoons a week. The public continued to speculate
about Diana and Prince Charles who, at the time, were
meeting at secret locations including friends' houses.

1981

A royal engagement

The engagement was officially announced at 11am on 24th February 1981, and Lady Diana and Prince Charles posed happily in the grounds of Buckingham Palace. He had proposed to her on 6th February, at the Palace, after a private supper and she accepted immediately. The engagement ring, supplied by Garrard's, the royal jewellers, was a large oval sapphire surrounded by fourteen diamonds and set in eighteen-carat white gold, and cost a princely £28,500. The Royal Family gave her a diamond and emerald pendant depicting the emblem of the Prince of Wales, which had previously belonged to Queen Mary.

First official function

Diana was immediately moved to Clarence House and then to Buckingham Palace, until the day of the wedding. It was soon time for her to attend her first official function and in March she accompanied Prince Charles to a recital in Goldsmiths Hall *(above left)*. She wore a revealing strapless silk taffeta gown and, on arrival, Prince Charles proudly told waiting photographers, 'You won't believe what's coming next' as she stepped out of the car.
Above top: Later that month Diana travelled to Sandown to watch Prince Charles ride in the Horse and Hound Grand Military Gold Cup. He was unseated a mile from the finish but fortunately came away relatively unscathed.
Above: Diana at Sandown with Charles's friend, Andrew Parker Bowles.

Living at Highgrove

In May, Diana and Prince Charles made an official visit to Tetbury in Gloucestershire to open a new operating theatre at the local hospital (Left). After their marriage, the royal couple would live nearby at Highgrove, a nine-bedroomed Georgian house built in 1796 for John Paul Paul. The Duchy of Cornwall had purchased it in 1980 as a private country residence for the Prince of Wales. During the months leading up to the wedding, Diana oversaw the refurbishment of the house while Charles focused on the gardens and surrounding land. The people of Tetbury presented them with two large ornamental gates as a wedding present so they would have greater security and privacy.

Wedding preparations

Above: On 11th June, Charles and Diana visited St Paul's Cathedral. Charles had specifically requested that they be married at the Cathedral, where he preferred the acoustics and architecture to those of the more traditional Westminster Abbey. The organisation of the wedding was in the hands of the Lord Chamberlain and was to be on a mammoth scale. Eleven carriages would be used, with three thousand policemen and three thousand soldiers lining the route. Television companies planned the largest-ever outside broadcasting event.

Right: A quiet moment during a polo match for the bride-to-be, a month before her wedding.

Polo-playing Prince

Prince Charles was a very committed polo player and Diana often accompanied him to matches. The weekend prior to their wedding, he played in a match at Guards Polo Club, organised by Major Ronald Ferguson (who also managed Charles's polo team). Diana spent much of the time talking excitedly to his daughter Sarah, already a good friend. One of the best-kept secrets before the wedding was the design of Diana's dress. To make it, she had selected the Emmanuels, who had created the black taffeta evening dress for her first public engagement. Her final choice was a fairy-tale confection made with forty-five feet of ivory silk taffeta.

The marriage service

Prince Charles and the twenty-year-old Lady Diana Spencer were married on 29th July 1981, a perfect summer's day. Prince Charles rode with his supporter, Prince Andrew, in an open carriage, while Diana shared the famous Glass Coach with her father, Earl Spencer. As she emerged from the coach at the steps to the Cathedral, the waiting public were finally able to see the stunning dress with its twenty-five-foot train. It had been made by one seamstress, Mrs Nina Missetzis, working in a locked room, and had ten thousand pearls and mother-of-pearl sequins hand-sewn onto the bodice. Together, Diana and her father made the three-and-a-half-minute walk down the aisle, accompanied by Jeremiah Clarke's *Trumpet Voluntary*. Her father was very shaky after a recent stroke, but was determined to give her away. Charles and Diana were married by the Archbishop of Canterbury, Dr. Robert Runcie, who pronounced, 'This is the stuff of which fairy tales are made.'

Newlyweds

The service was relayed outside, and the moment after their vows were made, jubilant applause could be heard echoing through the surrounding streets. In their nervousness, Diana had muddled Charles's names and he had agreed to share her worldly goods but not his own. Diana's wedding ring was made from a nugget of Welsh gold mined in 1923 and previously used for the wedding rings belonging to the Queen Mother, the Queen, Princess Margaret and Princess Anne. At the end of the service, the newly married couple emerged from the west door of St. Paul's to be greeted by cheering crowds.

The procession route

An estimated one million people lined the procession route back to Buckingham Palace, while approximately 750 million watched around the world. Thousands had camped out in the streets overnight, revelling in the spirit of the all-night party. As Charles and Diana rode through the streets in their open carriage, the crowds roared in delight.

1981

The balcony at Buckingham Palace

As the procession finished, barriers were moved and well-wishers poured down the Mall to surround Buckingham Palace. Just after one o'clock the doors to the balcony opened and Charles and Diana stepped out, to be greeted by a huge and appreciative crowd. The atmosphere was electric and the cheering grew louder and louder; finally, in response to persuasive chants, Charles kissed his bride. After the wedding breakfast, the couple left for Waterloo Station in a carriage festooned with twenty silver heart-shaped balloons and a gaudily decorated 'Just Married' sign, courtesy of Princes Andrew and Edward.

Honeymooners

From Waterloo, Charles and Diana travelled to Broadlands, home of the late Lord Mountbatten. They spent three lazy, secluded days here and then Prince Charles piloted an RAF Andover of the Queen's Flight to Gibraltar, where they were to board the Royal Yacht *Britannia*. For two weeks, the couple sailed around the Mediterranean, accompanied by a crew of 277, plus the band of the Royal Marines. After the cruise, they flew to Lossiemouth in Scotland to spend a month at Balmoral, along with other members of the Royal Family, there for the traditional summer break.

Left and left below: At Balmoral, the newlyweds strolled along the banks of the River Dee, deeply suntanned and holding hands. When asked about married life they both said coyly they could 'highly recommend it'.

At the end of October, the Prince and Princess of Wales embarked on an official three-day tour of Wales, their own principality. It was on this tour that Diana's immense popularity with the public was first noticed. Wherever they went, the waiting crowds were desperate to see her and were entranced by her informality. Traditional royal handshakes were not her style – she wanted to reach out spontaneously to touch people and cuddle children. She was an instant hit.

Below: Diana meets some of the waiting crowds at Haverfordwest.

Mum-to-be

Some people had noticed how pale Diana had been looking during the Welsh tour and on 5th November her pregnancy was announced, with their first baby due the following summer. From early on in the pregnancy, she suffered from very debilitating morning sickness and as a result, many public engagements had to be cancelled.

Left: Diana and Prince Andrew arrive at the Royal Opera House to watch a performance of the ballet *Romeo and Juliet*.

Below: Girlish and demure, Diana attended a function at the National Film Theatre with Prince Charles to celebrate the twenty-fifth anniversary of the London Film Festival.

Left below: Diana stands on the balcony overlooking the Cenotaph with King Olaf of Norway, Princess Alice and the Queen Mother.

1982

Planning the birth

From a very early stage in the pregnancy, Charles and Diana had decided that rather than follow royal tradition and have their baby at one of the official royal residences, she would give birth in the private Lindo Wing at St. Mary's Hospital, Paddington. Diana was a firm believer in natural childbirth and exercised regularly, taking breathing and relaxation lessons from a very experienced midwife, in readiness for the labour.

Left: As the pregnancy advanced, Diana resumed royal duties and in January she accompanied Charles on a visit to the Dick Sheppard School in Tulse Hill.

Below left and below: The royal couple arrive at Westminster Abbey for the Royal College of Music Centenary Service.

Kensington Palace

For the first ten months of married life, Charles and Diana's London base was a flat in Buckingham Palace, while an apartment in Kensington Place was restored and refurbished for them. They were finally able to move there in May, only weeks before their baby was due.

Above left: After attending the charity performance of *Little Foxes* at the Victoria Palace Theatre, Diana met Elizabeth Taylor backstage.

Above right: On a visit to open the Albany Community Centre in Deptford, South East London, Diana was told by a mother of five-year-old twins that, however many books you read about children, you don't actually learn until you have them.

Left: Three weeks before her due date, Diana was at Smith's Lawn to see Prince Charles play polo.

Welcome Prince William

Left: Prince William was born at 9.03pm on 21st June, weighing 7lb 1oz. As planned, he was delivered at St. Mary's, with Prince Charles present throughout the birth. It had been a long, sixteen-hour labour and when Prince Charles emerged from the hospital at 11pm that night he confessed, 'I'm overwhelmed by it. It was a very grown-up experience'. The Queen ordered a forty-one gun salute both in Hyde Park and at the Tower of London. Diana decided to leave the hospital at 6pm the following evening, smiling happily to the waiting crowds. Ten days later, on 1st July, she would celebrate her twenty-first birthday.

Below left and below right: On 26th July, Diana attended her first public engagement after William's birth: the Falkland Islands Thanksgiving Service at St Paul's Cathedral. William had been born the day after the war ended.

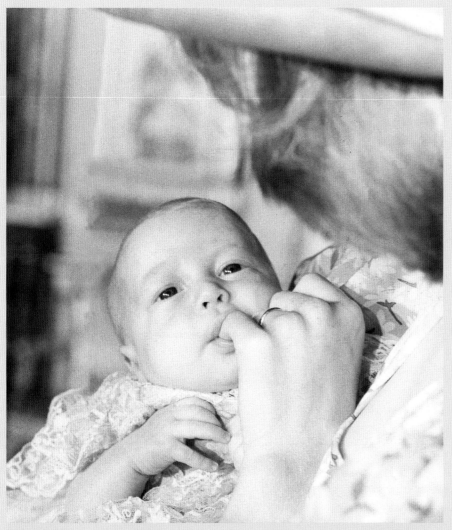

William Arthur Philip Louis

Left: William was christened on 4th August in the Music Room at Buckingham Palace. This date was chosen to coincide with the Queen Mother's eighty-second birthday. The Archbishop of Canterbury, Dr. Robert Runcie, led the baptismal service and the long list of godparents included former King Constantine of Greece; Lady Susan Hussey, one of the Queen's senior Ladies-in-Waiting; Princess Alexandra; Lord Romsey, Lord Mountbatten's grandson; Sir Laurens van der Post, and the Duchess of Westminster. Following royal custom, William wore a robe of Honiton lace, first used for Victoria and Albert's babies, and was baptised with water from the River Jordan, a tradition that reaches back to the Crusades.

Below left: Diana attended the wedding of former flatmate Carolyn Pride to William Bartholomew.

Below right: After opening an extension to the Royal School for the Blind in Leatherhead, Surrey, Diana stopped to talk to the children who came to greet her.

Representing the Royal Family

The Royal Family were at Balmoral when they learnt of the death of Princess Grace of Monaco in a car accident. Diana had previously met her on her first public engagement. She had been very nervous and Princess Grace had taken the time to reassure her and give her confidence – an act that Diana had always remembered. Diana was keen to attend the funeral and the Queen allowed her to represent the Royal Family on her own. *Above left:* In November, Queen Beatrix and Prince Claus of the Netherlands made a state visit to Britain. They were welcomed at Westminster Pier by several members of the Royal Family including the Prince and Princess of Wales. A two-day tour of Wales was scheduled for the royal couple the same month and the visits included Aberdovey (*above right*) and Wrexham (*left*).

A hardworking royal

Above: A visit to the wreck of the *Mary Rose* in Portsmouth. Although Diana did not always find it easy to adapt to protocol, she began to settle into life as a member of the Royal Family.

Right: Accompanying Prince Charles to the premiere of the film *Gandhi*. The presence of the Princess ensured that the photographers and fashion writers turned out in force.

Below: On a visit to the Department of Health and Social Security, Diana was greeted by MP Norman Fowler and staff on a twenty-four- hour strike over alleged under-manning of offices. The strikers, however, deemed her visit to be charity work and allowed her through their picket line.

Below right: Just prior to Christmas, Diana visited the Royal Marsden Hospital in Fulham, where she spent an hour meeting staff and chatting to cancer patients.

And baby came too

The year began with Charles and Diana taking their first skiing holiday together in Lech, Austria. At times, Diana found it difficult to cope with the persistent paparazzi who followed her wherever she went. At home, William was now six months old. Diana adored him: nanny Barbara Barnes cared for him but Diana spent as much time with him as she could. She missed her son terribly on the Austrian holiday and vowed from that moment to avoid any unnecessary separations. His parents soon found themselves abbreviating his name to Wills.

Left: In February, Diana visited Nightingale Home for the Elderly in South West London.

In March, Charles and Diana embarked on a six-week tour of Australia and New Zealand and at Diana's insistence William came with them. She knew that Charles had endured months of separation from his parents and neither of them was prepared to leave William for this long. Nanny Barbara Barnes accompanied them and looked after William at a base in New South Wales, while his parents flew across the continent, completing a gruelling schedule. Charles and Diana saw their son in between official engagements, and to mark the occasion William crawled for the first time. Diana was an instant hit with the Australians, who came out in their thousands to see her, and as Charles guided her through the protocol of official life, her confidence began to grow.

Below left: At a charity ball in Sydney, Charles whisked Diana around the dance floor as she pleaded with him to slow down – they were clearly enjoying themselves.

Below: Charles and Diana attended a luncheon at the Dorchester Hotel in aid of the Leukaemia Research Fund and the Injured National Hunt Jockey Fund.

Summer visits

Below: The Prince and Princess of Wales in fancy dress at Fort Edmonton, Canada. They had attended a costume barbecue where guests dressed in styles from the Gold Rush age. Diana's dress – earlier worn by actress Francesca Annis when she played Lillie Langtry in a TV drama series – was very heavily boned and apparently quite a relief to take off at the end of the evening.

Below right: At the premiere of the new Bond film *Octopussy,* Diana, who appeared to have lost yet more weight, met the movie's producer, Cubby Broccoli.

Above right: The Variety Club Sunshine Coach luncheon was held at the Guildhall in July, with Diana as guest of honour.

Above: Meeting the crowds in Tavistock, Devon.

Honouring the Spencer family

Below: In July, Diana opened the new Admissions Unit of St. Andrew's Hospital in Northampton. The building was named Spencer House, in honour of the Spencer family's long service to the hospital. She attended the ceremony with her father and stepmother, Lord and Lady Spencer.

Above and top: The Queen's Theatre, Shaftesbury Avenue was the venue for a charity performance of Noel Coward's *Hay Fever*. Diana arrived wearing an exquisite silk evening gown that drew gasps from the waiting crowds.

Above right: After the performance, Diana talked to actress Penelope Keith. By now, features on Diana's clothes and style were regularly appearing in newspapers and magazines. She had brought glamour to the Royal Family and her clothes and hairstyles were assiduously copied. She chose British designers to support and promote the country's fashion industry.

Below right: Charles and Diana at Stoke Mandeville Hospital.

1983

Proud parents

Left: William at eighteen months, in the gardens at Kensington Palace. He showed a natural curiosity for the world and had already established a reputation for being a mischievous toddler, earning the nickname of Wombat.

Left: Despite the rain, Diana met the waiting crowds outside the Asian Centre in Walthamstow in November.

Below left: Children at the West Indian Family Centre in Brixton chatted and sang to Diana. They were delighted when she broke into an impromptu calypso dance.

Below: As the year drew to a close, Diana attended the Dominion Theatre to watch a production of *Carmen* by the Welsh National Opera.

Expecting again

Diana's second pregnancy was announced on St. Valentine's Day, with the next baby due in September. Diana later revealed that she and Charles had a very close relationship in the months before Harry's birth.

Above left: At a Jewish Welfare Board dinner held at the Guildhall, Diana was presented with flowers and a tiny rocking chair for the new baby.

Left and above right: As she visited the knitting factory of T W Kempton Ltd in Leicester, employees showed her some of the baby clothes they made.

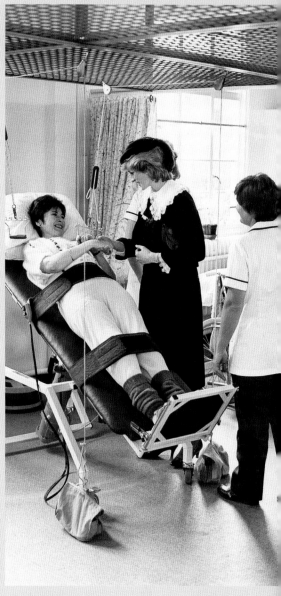

Smiling through

During her second pregnancy Diana again suffered from morning sickness, which often lasted throughout the day.

As she opened a £2 million spinal injuries unit at the Royal National Orthopaedic Hospital in Stanmore, she looked very queasy at times. However, she continued to laugh and joke with patients and the waiting crowds.

Left and above: The Royal Marsden Hospital in Sutton welcomed her on a cold February morning.

A very popular Princess

Above right: After a tour of the Royal Doulton factory in Burslem, Stoke-on-Trent, Diana received many good wishes from the crowds. In contrast to her first pregnancy, when she wore over-sized maternity clothes, Diana presented a much more slimline shape the second time around. She put on less weight and wore clothes that concealed rather than accentuated her pregnancy. She was again planning to have the baby at St. Mary's in Paddington.

Above left and left: The pearly King and Princess of Deptford in South East London greeted her as she visited the Albany Centre in the town.

Gifts for William and the new baby

Top: A crowd of ten thousand gathered to watch the Prince and Princess of Wales unveil a memorial to Lewis Carroll in the middle of Warrington. The fourteen-year-old son of the licensee of the Mad Hatter pub presented her with two specially bound editions of *Alice in Wonderland* for Prince William and the new baby.

Above: After officially opening Callard and Bowser's new £8 million sweet factory near Bridgend, Diana then toured the plant.

Left: On a walkabout in Glastonbury.

1984

Charles and Diana at the movies

Left: At the charity premiere of *Indiana Jones and the Temple of Doom*, Diana and Charles greeted members of the film's cast after the screening.

Below: Although Diana preferred pop music to opera, the couple had the opportunity to meet tenor Luciano Pavarotti, who became one of her favourite performers.

Bottom: In July, Diana attended the Royal Tournament at Earls Court with Prince Charles.

Last engagements before the birth

Right: Diana was a keen spectator at Cirencester when she watched Charles's polo team win 7-6.

Below right: A visit to King's College Hospital in the last few weeks before her second baby was due.

Below: Four weeks before the birth and two weeks before her twenty-third birthday, Diana had flown to Scotland to join the Royal Family at Balmoral. Her uncle Lord Fermoy had just died and she was visibly upset.

Prince Harry is born

Prince Henry Charles Albert David was born on Saturday 15th September weighing 6lb 14oz. Diana had gone into labour that morning while at Windsor and was immediately driven to the hospital, with a police escort. The following day, Prince Charles brought William to see his new brother, who would be soon known as Harry.
Left: Members of the public and the media waited outside St. Mary's all day to hear news of the impending birth.
Below left: Diana left the hospital with the newborn prince on Sunday 16th September to return to Kensington Palace.

Back in the public eye

Above left and above: Diana resumed her public engagements soon after Harry's birth and in November visited the Dr Barnardo Centre in Newham, East London. She met staff and children to find out more about the various activities in which they were involved.

Right: A visit to the Children's Centre, Ealing, in November.

In December, Prince Harry was christened Henry Charles Albert David at St. George's Chapel, Windsor. His godparents were Lady Celia Vestey, Lady Sarah Armstrong Jones, Carolyn Bartholomew (Diana's former flatmate), Prince Andrew, Bryan Organ (royal artist) and Gerald Ward.

President of Dr Barnardo's

Left and bottom: Princess Diana was President of Dr Barnardo's and in February made a visit to their headquarters in Tanners Lane, Ilford. She took a great interest in the work of the charity and was very moved by the plight of some of the children. As she left, she was cheered by the youngsters awaiting fostering or adoption in the Barnardo's Village next door.

Below: When Phil Collins gave a concert in aid of the Prince of Wales Trust, he met Diana afterwards and gave her two tiny tour jackets for William and Harry.

Bottom left: A very enthusiastic greeting from members of the Broadwater Farm Youth Association.

Determined to get there despite the snow

Left: The Princess had made a personal request to visit the Foundation for the Study of Infant Deaths at Peterhouse College, Cambridge, and was not deterred by the several inches of snow that fell on the day scheduled for her visit. She told one of the founder members, 'I'm a mother – that's why I couldn't get here fast enough.'

A Home Office pathologist had recently claimed that most cot death victims were smothered by mothers or fathers, causing immense distress to bereaved parents. Diana was determined to give her support, and bereaved parents were very touched by her visit and sympathetic words.

Below: Diana takes time out from royal duties to attend the private wedding of a friend.

Below left: A smiling Diana on a visit to Cirencester Police Station.

Continuing the work for Barnardo's

Left: In March, Diana carried out her first public engagement for Dr. Barnardo's, now renamed simply Barnardo's, when she attended a fashion gala in London. She wore a sensational silver pleated dress designed by Bruce Oldfield, a former Barnardo's boy, who organised the event.

Right: An opportunity for Diana again to meet Dame Kiri Te Kanawa, at a gala concert in aid of the Westminster Children's Hospital, at the Banqueting Hall, Whitehall. Dame Kiri had sung Handel's *Let the Bright Seraphim* at Diana's marriage to Prince Charles four years previously.

Dropping in for a chat!

Above left: Diana says farewell to a resident after stopping for a chat through his window, during a visit to the Poolmead Centre of the Royal National Institute for the Deaf in Bath.

Left: At times, critics claimed that she was too extravagant with her wardrobe but this Bruce Oldfield dress had another outing for the premiere of *A View to a Kill* at the Odeon, Leicester Square.

Above: Unperturbed by the rain, a smiling Diana met crowds at the Ravenswood Foundation at Crowthorne in Buckinghamshire, a centre for the care of people with learning difficulties.

Below: A delighted princess watched her husband's polo team beat Brazil 6-5 in the Silver Jubilee Cup. Charles was playing for the England II polo team at the Guards Polo Club in Windsor.

Live Aid

Left: In July, Diana opened a new wing at Lincoln County Hospital. That same month, the Prince and Princess attended the Live Aid concert, a concept dreamed up by pop singer Bob Geldof. The sixteen-hour event was held simultaneously at Wembley Stadium and JFK Stadium in Philadelphia, to raise money for the starving in Ethiopia. The concert was seen by 1.5 billion people and eventually raised $40 million through donations and phone pledges. Diana was seen bopping along to the music, fully behind the initiative.

Below: Princess Diana and Prince Andrew attended the marriage of the Hon. Carolyn Herbert to John Warren. The wedding was held at Highclere Castle in Berkshire.

Below left: Diana opened The International Stoke Mandeville Games at the end of July.

Above: Diana adopts a nautical look for a visit to the Isle of Wight in May.

Left: The Prince and Princess of Wales visited the King's Troop Royal Horse Artillery in St. John's Wood, London. In April, Charles and Diana were on an official tour of Italy that began in Sardinia. During an audience with Pope John Paul II, Diana ensured she was appropriately dressed in an ankle-length black dress and black lace mantilla. William and Harry were flown out to join their parents when they reached Venice, so they could all enjoy a short Mediterranean cruise, aboard *Britannia*.

Her 'beloved boys'

Left and below left: The family boarded the Royal Yacht *Britannia* in August, to join other members of the royal party as they cruised around the Western Isles. At the end of the holiday they would all travel to Scotland for the traditional stay at Balmoral, until October.

Below: At the age of three it was time for William to make the transition into childhood. Traditionally, children in the Royal Family had been educated at home at this early age, but Diana wanted William to mix with his peers and make his own friends, so his parents eventually chose Miss Mynors' kindergarten in London's Notting Hill Gate. After much preparation, including the installation of additional security, William arrived for his first day at school in September. It was a very happy school with three classes, each with twelve children.

Solo visits

Left and above: On a solo visit to a military base in West Berlin in the autumn it was clear that Diana was gradually carrying out more engagements on her own.

Top left and top right: During a visit to St. Joseph's Hospice in Hackney, East London, Diana took the opportunity to joke with patients.

In October, Sir Alastair Burnet interviewed the Prince and Princess of Wales. Twenty million viewers watched the programme as they talked frankly and happily about their lives together.

Tour of Australia and the USA

Left: The royal couple took the opportunity to kiss when the cup was awarded after a polo match, at Werribee Park in Australia.

Below right and bottom left: Diana again set the fashion trends when she attended the races in Australia on Melbourne Cup Day. When the tour reached the USA, the Prince and Princess attended a White House dinner in Washington where Diana danced with both *Saturday Night Fever* star John Travolta and actor Clint Eastwood. Prince Charles, meanwhile, was waltzing with the First Lady, Nancy Reagan.

Below left: Despite being celebrated as a fashion icon around the world for her fabulous sense of style, she had to endure criticism from Australian fashion writers, who claimed that this outfit was dowdy and that she had saved her best for the States.

Bottom right: On their return from the tour, the Prince and Princess attended the Birthday Ball at the Albert Hall in aid of the Birthright charity. Her brother Charles, Viscount Althorp, greeted her.

Uptown Girl

Above left and left: Wearing a stunning, backless, crushed velvet evening gown, Diana met Stephen Spielberg after the premiere of his film *Back to the Future*, at the Empire Theatre.

Above: A fabulous shot of the Princess as she arrived at the Odeon, Leicester Square for the premiere of *Santa Claus*.

Diana had secretly been working with dancer Wayne Sleep to surprise her husband. Charles was due at a Royal Gala performance at Covent Garden and she wanted to appear on stage performing a dance for him. After numerous clandestine rehearsals at Kensington Palace, the Prince and Princess attended the performance. Just before the end she appeared, dancing to Billy Joel's 'Uptown Girl'. Charles was speechless and she received eight curtain calls from a delighted audience!

Below right and below left: On a visit to the Bentham Estate Tenants Association in Islington, she turned down the offer of a sweet from one of the four-year-olds. She had been touring the pre-school playgroup and the Bean Club for Youth.

Working with deaf people

Left: In her role as President of the Royal Academy of Music, Diana and Charles attended a choral concert at the Royal Academy in Marylebone Road, central London.

Above: At a visit to the Deaf Centre in Northampton, Diana was put through her paces on the snooker table. Much to the fifteen-year-old's delight, Diana potted a red straight away. Afterwards she was able to answer several silent questions from the children as she put her lip-reading skills to the test. Most wanted to ask her about Princes William and Harry.

Middle left: On a visit to Ridgway House Retirement Home for the Elderly in Towcester, Diana stopped to talk to schoolchildren outside.

Below left: When Diana visited the West Midlands, members of the Litchfield Deaf Church performed the hymn *God Be in my Head* using sign language. The Chaplain for the Deaf, Father George Moody, greeted her.

Below: Meeting children and well-wishers at the Markfield project, North London.

Wedding bells for Prince Andrew and Fergie

Left: Prince Charles held a pre-wedding dinner for close members of the family, prior to Prince Andrew's marriage to Sarah Ferguson on 23rd July. Sarah and Diana famously dressed up as policewomen and tried to gatecrash Andrew's stag night at Annabel's night club.

During the previous year, Diana had played cupid as a romance between Prince Andrew and Sarah Ferguson began to develop. Diana and Sarah had always been close friends, lunching together regularly. After Sarah was invited to Windsor for Royal Ascot, Prince Andrew asked her to join him at Balmoral for the summer break. She accompanied Charles and Diana for a skiing holiday in Klosters and for once, media attention was away from Diana as the paparazzi rushed to photograph Sarah Ferguson. Prince Andrew proposed to her later that month.

Middle left: On a wet day in May, a suitably prepared Diana visited the Agricultural Show in Ipswich.

Below left: Diana arrives at the Empire Theatre, Leicester Square.

Below: With other representatives of the Royal Family, Charles and Diana met the President of the Federal Republic of Germany and Freifrau von Weizsacker who were in Britian for a four-day state visit. Their arrival at Victoria Station was followed by a carriage procession to Buckingham Palace.

Bottom right: When Diana and Charles arrived at St. George's Chapel, Windsor, Charles was wearing a sling having accidentally hit a finger while hammering in a stake in the garden.

Diana at the ballet

Left: In her role as Patron of the British Deaf Association, Diana arrived at the Royal Opera House for a performance of *Ivan the Terrible* by the Bolshoi Ballet.
Below left: Applauding the stars at the London Standard Ballet Awards, held at the London Coliseum.

Towards the end of a busy year, the Prince and Princess toured the Arabian Gulf. Diana was invited to King Fahd's palace in Saudi Arabia but was not allowed to dine with the men. The Sultan of Oman was very generous with his gifts, giving Diana priceless jewels and Charles an Aston Martin.
Below: Diana was asked to open a new gallery at the National Maritime Museum in Greenwich, called 'Discovery and Sea Power 1450-1700'.
Bottom: Greetings for the elegant Princess as she arrived for a charity luncheon in aid of Save the Baby.

Getting into the spirit

Below left: As Charles and Diana toured Pinewood Studios to see the making of the new James Bond film, *The Living Daylights*, the Princess had the opportunity to break a prop bottle over Charles's head!

Left: Diana attending a screening of *The Mission* for the charity Birthright, at the Empire, Leicester Square.

Below: Accompanied by the Archbishop of Canterbury, Dr. Robert Runcie, Diana walked to the Carol Service at Canterbury Cathedral.

Against the elements

Above left: On a windy day in January, Diana left the Help the Aged headquarters in Clerkenwell. Prince William had just started his pre-prep education at Wetherby School in Notting Hill, just five minutes from Kensington Palace. William was to settle in happily. His start at Wetherby coincided with a change of nanny, with Ruth Wallace taking over the role.

Above: The following week Diana opened a new unit at the Whitefield School for Deaf Children in Walthamstow, London.

Left: The Princess again set a trend when she attended a concert given by the London Philharmonic at the Royal Festival Hall, accompanying children from the London Borough of Tower Hamlets. The black and gold tassels on her stockings were soon noticed and copied.

Rumours about Charles and Diana's marriage were starting to increase as they attended more and more functions separately. Sharp-eyed members of the media noticed the tension between them and the absence of the warmth and devotion that they had once shared.

Musicals and ballet

Above left: The Princess sported fashionable leather trousers to attend a performance of *The Phantom of the Opera* at Her Majesty's Theatre.

Left: Lionel Richie presented her with leather bomber jackets for the princes, decorated with their names. She was at the Lionel Richie concert at Wembley Arena in support of the British Institute of Florence and the Prince's Trust.

Above: World Health Day in April was marked by a Rubella Council luncheon at Marlborough House.

Family connections

Above: Diana with Harrods boss
Mohamed Al Fayed. He was a close friend
of Earl Spencer and Diana had known
him since she was eight. They watched as
Charles scored four goals when his
Windsor Park polo team beat the Guards.
The match was organised by Al Fayed and
they were playing for the Harrods Trophy.
£30,000 was also raised for the Malcolm
Sargent Cancer Fund for Children.
Left: A bright pink bow tie dressed up her
suit when she went to the London
Hippodrome to see the jazz ballet
Nightcreature.

Happy birthday to you!

Above: Diana celebrated her twenty-sixth birthday at Wimbledon, where she watched a riveting match on the centre court between Lendl and Leconte. She was given a rousing chorus of 'Happy Birthday' by fellow spectators. Watching with her were Princess Michael of Kent and Mrs Catherine Soames, a close friend with whom Diana played tennis regularly. The Princess attended Wimbledon as often as she could and was always an enthusiastic supporter.

Right: Tree-planting duty at Sovereign's Parade, Sandhurst. Diana's military-style suit was designed by Catherine Walker. On a tour of Spain in April the Prince and Princess were guests of King Juan Carlos and his wife, Queen Sofia. At the end of the tour, Diana flew home alone, while Charles had a brief holiday in Italy.

Below: Al Fayed then laid on a tea party for fifty children suffering from cancer, many of whom had a very short time to live. The children were overjoyed to meet the Prince and Princess of Wales but it was a very emotional occasion for all involved.

The new Bond movie

Having visited Pinewood Studios during the making of the film, the Prince and Princess attended the premiere of *The Living Daylights* at the Odeon, Leicester Square. Diana met the new James Bond, Timothy Dalton (*right*) and his leading lady, Maryam d'Abo.

It was during 1987 that Diana became determined to direct her energies towards a more fulfilling cause. She was a devoted mother and supportive wife, but wanted to use her compassion and caring nature to make a difference to other people's lives. During the year she realised that the Aids charities needed help and visited the first clinic at the Middlesex Hospital, meeting nine men dying of Aids-related illnesses, publicly shaking hands with a patient. Overnight, she highlighted the help they needed and began to dispel the myths that surrounded the virus.

Meeting the former Beatles

Above left: After the Prince's Trust Concert at Wembley in June, Diana was introduced to former Beatles, George Harrison and Ringo Starr.
Above: A stunning princess arrived at Charleston Manor in Sussex for a function in aid of the London City Ballet and the Purcell School.
Left: Diana joined several other members of the Royal Family to greet the King of Monaco at a formal reception at Claridge's.

Freeman of the City

On 22nd July, Diana addressed four hundred guests at the Guildhall. She had just been made a Freeman of the City and was noticeably nervous before she began to speak. First she had to swear an oath of allegiance to the Queen, before making her own brief speech.

Above right: As Diana spoke in response to being made a Freeman of the City, she was watched by (left to right): the Lady Mayoress of London; Prince Charles; Lady Raine Spencer; her father, Lord Spencer; her brother, Charles Spencer, Viscount Althorp; her mother, Mrs Frances Shand Kydd and her grandmother Ruth, Lady Fermoy. Afterwards she made another speech at a lunch held at the Mansion House.

Below: A quieter day for Diana at Ascot Races. In August, she and Charles were once again guests of the King and Queen of Spain, this time for a family holiday at the Spanish Royal Family's villa in Majorca. After the holiday, Prince Harry followed in his brother's footsteps and started at Miss Mynors' kindergarten in Notting Hill. He began at the school the day after his third birthday.

The Princess of Wales Conservatory

Above left: Diana unveiled the commemorative plaque for the new Princess of Wales conservatory at the Royal Botanic Gardens in Kew. Designed by architect Gordon Wilson, it was billed as the world's largest conservatory.

Above: Often overcome with laughter, Diana had a wonderful evening at the Whitehall Theatre watching a charity performance of *The Importance of Being Earnest*. The production starred Hinge and Bracket and afterwards she met Dame Hilda Bracket, alias Patrick Fyffe, who played Lady Bracknell.

Left: Supporting a safety campaign to prevent children from swallowing household chemicals, Diana was greeted by children at Sulivan Primary School in Fulham, London.

Below: A trip down memory lane when Diana returned to visit her old school – West Heath in Sevenoaks. She was accompanied by her two sisters, Jane and Sarah, and during the visit was presented with flowers by pupil Anna Nevill.

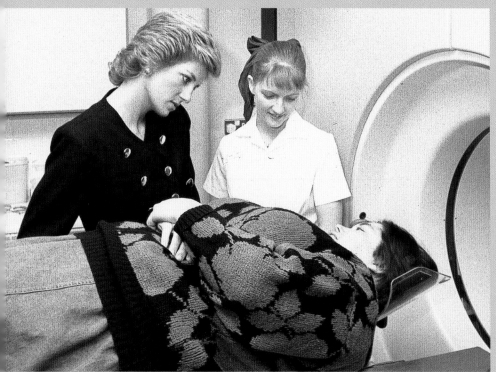

Patron of the ballet

Above left: As patron of the London City Ballet, Diana attended a charity performance of the ballet *Talking Steps*. The evening was organised to raise money towards a minibus for the elderly.

Left: She was invited to open a new X-ray department at the National Hospital for Nervous Diseases. Compassionate as ever, in the CT scanner room she made time to talk to a patient and radiologists.

Above: A much shorter hairstyle and a purple off-the-shoulder gown for the charity premiere of *The Last Emperor*, nominated for nine Oscars. The evening raised more than £100,000 for the Prince's Trust.

The Prince and Princess toured Thailand in February and the enthusiastic locals soon christened her 'Thai Di'. She again flew home alone while Charles went on safari with friends in Tanzania.

Tragedy at Klosters

Left: In March, Major Hugh Lindsay, a great friend of Prince Charles, was killed in a skiing accident at Klosters. Prince Charles narrowly avoided being hurt as well. The Major's body was flown back to RAF Northolt in Middlesex and the coffin was carried from the plane by a guard of honour. Grim-faced, Princess Diana and the Duchess of York, also on the skiing holiday, attended the sad occasion.

Below left: Zara Phillips and Prince William leave St. George's Chapel with Diana after the traditional Easter Sunday service.

Below: Sarah, Duchess of York, was expecting her first baby when she joined Diana and other members of the Royal Family to welcome the King of Norway at Windsor Castle, for a state visit.

Wet Wet Wet!

Below: After a rock concert for the Prince's Trust at the Royal Albert Hall, two members of the band Wet Wet Wet were introduced to the Princess.

Below left: A warm smile from Diana at the opening of a drug rehabilitation centre in Andover, Hampshire.

Above: Strapless and sensational at the premiere of the film *Crocodile Dundee*.

Left: Diana chose an immaculately tailored dinner suit for a fund-raising greyhound meeting at Wembley – which only served to emphasise her femininity.

1988

Royal wedding

Right: In July, Princess Alexandra's son James Ogilvy married Julia Rawlinson at the Church of St. Mary the Virgin in Saffron Walden, Essex. Diana arrived with Princess Margaret.

Below right: At the opening of the Barbican Fitness Centre, Diana met swimmer Duncan Goodhew (*centre*) and dancer Wayne Sleep. After he had tutored her for her debut dance at Covent Garden, Diana had remained good friends with the ballet dancer.

Below: A radiant Princess in sea-faring mood.

'Auntie Diana'

Left: Sarah, Duchess of York gave birth to her first daughter, Beatrice, on 11th August at the Portland Hospital, London. Diana was one of her first visitors, along with Princes William and Harry.

Right: Diana surrounded by well-wishers at St. Catherine's Hospice in Crawley, Surrey.

Working with Aids charities

Above: Boxer Frank Bruno had Diana in stitches when she attended a London reception held by the British Sports Association for the disabled in aid of the disabled competitors and officials who would be travelling to the Paralympics in Seoul, South Korea. Afterwards he commented, 'She's a very beautiful lady'.

Left: Newspaper proprietor, Robert Maxwell greeted Diana as she arrived at the Guildhall for the launch of the National Aids Trust.

Below left: Another favourite dress is given a second outing at the Annual National Service for Seafarers at St. Paul's Cathedral, London.

Below: The Annual General Meeting of one of her favourite charities, Barnado's. As President, Diana had recently been filmed visiting a family fostering three children in Tottenham. The five-minute clip was part of a documentary showing people how under-privileged children could be helped in the right environment. Diana had stayed to talk to the family long after the filming had finished.

Patron of the Child Accident Prevention Trust

Left and below: In October, Diana attended the Annual General Meeting of the Child Accident Prevention Trust. At the meeting she raised the issue of dangerous toys and asked everyone buying children Christmas gifts to ensure the toys were totally safe.

Below middle: In warmer conditions, Diana was at a Royal premiere at the Empire, Leicester Square. Afterwards, she met actor Warwick Davis.

Bottom: Joining the Queen Mother and the members of the Royal Family at Sandringham Parish Church for the Christmas Day Service.

Below left: In the Isle of Wight, she named a new customs boat at Cowes. The Vigilant was the first of a new breed of cutters that could use high speed and advanced radar and communications equipment to intercept drug smugglers.

Harry joins Wetherby School

Left: In January, Prince Harry followed William to Wetherby, his pre-prep school in Notting Hill. Teachers soon noticed Harry's natural academic ability and love of learning, which earned him a place in the top groups.

Below: The Prince and Princess leave after the school run.

Below left: At the launch of the British Lung Foundation 'Bike 89' in Hyde Park.

Crusade to end Aids prejudice

Above right: In baseball hat and cowboy boots, Diana left Wetherby School after dropping Harry at the start of the summer term. Charles and Diana toured Kuwait and the United Arab Emirates in March, again departing separately when their official duties were over; Diana returning to England and Charles painting in Saudi Arabia.

Above: Diana made a surprise visit to the Mayday Hospital in Thornton Heath to comfort survivors from the Purley rail crash. She met the driver of the train, who had broken both hips, and the youngest victim, aged four.

Right: Diana used every opportunity she could to counter the prejudice against Aids victims. During a visit to the Mildmay Mission Hospital in Bethnal Green, East London, she held hands with patients and sat down with them in the informal style that always endeared her to staff and patients. Earlier in the month she had cuddled a toddler in New York who was dying of an Aids-related illness, winning the hearts of the American people.

Return to Riddlesworth Hall

Above left: In April, Diana returned to her old school, Riddlesworth Hall in Norfolk. She was invited to open a new annexe, where pupil Stephen Keregari helped her unveil the commemorative plaque.

Left: Prince Harry rushes ahead to attend William's school concert at the Palace Theatre.

Above: The Princess arriving at the Savoy Hotel for the Floral Luncheon for Forces Workshops.

Flower festival
Above left: Diana and Cardinal
Basil Hume chatted happily at
the Festival of Flowers Service in
Westminster Abbey. Later she
greeted the crowds outside the
abbey. (*left*)
Above: A wry look from Diana as
she waited at Victoria Station
with Prince Charles and other
members of the Royal Family to
welcome the President of
Nigeria for a state visit.

Colonel-in-chief

Above left: As new colonel-in-chief to the 13th /18th Royal Hussars, Diana made her first visit to their barracks at Tidworth in Hampshire. The soldiers, known as 'The Lilywhites', presented the Princess with a bouquet, and she watched an exhibition as ten men lifted each other on their shoulders to form a human triangle.

Above: Diana struggled with a fountain pen during a visit to the ante-natal clinic at the Queen Elizabeth II hospital in Welwyn Garden City, Hertfordshire.

Left: A warm June evening as Diana was escorted by David Lloyd to a celebrity night organised at his tennis centre in Raynes Park.

Sports day star!

Above: After dispensing with her shoes, Diana cut a dashing figure as she managed a very creditable second place in the mothers' eighty-yard sprint at the annual Wetherby School sports day.

Above left: At the Chalfont Centre for Epilepsy, Diana helped a resident to cut her ninety-sixth birthday cake.

Left: Four-and-a-half-year-old Prince Harry attending the Easter Sunday service at St. George's Chapel, Windsor Castle with his mother.

Viscount Althorp marries

Above left: In September, Diana's brother Charles married Victoria Lockwood, a twenty-five-year-old model and the daughter of a civil aviation executive. The wedding took place on the Althorp Estate in Northamptonshire with Prince Harry as a pageboy. Diana arrived with William and Charles.
Above: Diana at the wedding with her mother, Mrs Frances Shand Kydd.
Left: On an unannounced private visit, Diana and Prince William rushed into the Motorfair at Earls Court. Their first stop was at the Ferrari stand to admire the new Testarossa, priced at £107,000.

Remembrance Day

Left and below: A sombre moment as Diana, wearing a military-style outfit in appropriate colours, laid a wreath at the Guards' Chapel in Wellington Barracks, London.
Bottom right: As newly-appointed president of the Royal Academy of Dramatic Art, Diana installed Sir John Gielgud as the academy's first honorary fellow, in recognition of his life's work.
Below left: Arriving for the Panasonic Sports Personality of the Year Award.

Lady in red

Above: At the royal premiere of *When Harry Met Sally*, American stars Billy Crystal and Meg Ryan were introduced to the Princess. The premiere, held at the Odeon in Leicester Square, raised £50,000 for Turning Point; the charity, of which Diana was patron, aimed at rehabilitating alcoholics and drug users.

On the November tour of Hong Kong, locals this time called her 'Diana Wong Fei', which meant 'Diana, royal concubine'. While Diana flew home alone, Charles cruised around the South China Sea.

Left: Red was always one of Diana's favourite colours and she made a striking figure in this outfit on a visit to RAF Wittering.

Below: Diana and Charles at 10 Downing Street, with Prime Minister Margaret Thatcher and her husband Denis.

Further work with Aids charities

Above left: After opening the Rodney Porter ward at St. Mary's Hospital in Paddington, Diana toured the hospital and was updated on its research programme. She then met patients and spent some time chatting to them. The new ward, financed jointly by the NHS and Aids charities, was to specialise in the treatment of Aids and carriers of the HIV virus. Diana had also made a very significant visit to Jakarta in November when she famously shook hands with people suffering from leprosy – once again she drove through all the myths and prejudice that could surround an illness.
Left: Unveiling a window at St. Albans Abbey.
Above: The annual walk to Sandringham Parish Church on Christmas Day.

Keeping fit with Fergie

Below left: During the Duchess of York's second pregnancy, Sarah regularly swam with Diana. Sarah and Prince Andrew's first daughter, Beatrice, was now eighteen months old and Sarah was determined not to gain the weight that she had put on in her first pregnancy. While spending the traditional Christmas and New Year at Sandringham they used a club near King's Lynn. After Eugenie was born, Diana continued to help her friend exercise to shift any excess pounds. Diana eventually asked fitness instructor Carolan Brown to be her own personal instructor. She would go to Kensington Palace so Diana could embark on an exercise programme in greater privacy. One of the first points she addressed was Diana's posture. She was 5 feet 10 inches tall and, consequently, had a tendency to stoop.

Left: Appropriately attired for a visit to the Shia Islamic Centre in Stanmore.

Below: In February, she launched the centenary year of the British Deaf Association.

Concern for the homeless

Below: Diana always showed concern for the plight of the homeless and visited a Day Centre for young homeless people in Adelaide Street, London. She was also very keen to show her sons the different lives that some people were forced to lead and in 1993 organised a secret visit for the boys to a night shelter run by a group of nuns.

Left: Protective glasses were needed during a visit to BT & D Technologies Ltd in Ipswich.

Above: At the premiere of *Steel Magnolias,* Diana met (left to right): Sally Field, Olympia Dukakis, Daryl Hannah and Julia Roberts.

State visit to Nigeria

Far left: Diana chose a dress in Nigeria's national colours for her arrival on a five-day visit, which began with a greeting by the president's wife, Madame Ankanobi. Prior to the visit, the Prince and Princess of Wales had had anti-typhoid and yellow fever inoculations. They toured in temperatures of 110° F.

Left: Laughter at the Metropolitan Police Driving School, Hendon. Later that year, ironically, she would be on the wrong side of the law when she was caught speeding one morning in High Street Kensington. She went through a pelican crossing red light at seven in the morning.

Virgin Islands holiday

Left: A spring break was spent with the boys in the Virgin Islands.

Above: A tanned Princess, on return from the holiday, met actor Sean Connery at the premiere of *The Hunt for Red October*.

Thoughtful Diana

Above left and above: After officially opening the Depaul Trust housing for homeless youths project, Diana spoke to Cardinal Hume and one of the young people involved.

Left: In temperatures that soared into the eighties, Diana made a visit to Lorne House, a hostel run by Turning Point, for those with drink and drug related problems. Instead of leaving as planned, she went to talk to a crowd in a nearby courtyard who had waited over an hour in the sweltering heat to see her.

Lunch with the Viscount

Below left and below right: She met her brother Charles, Viscount Althorp, for lunch at her favourite restaurant, San Lorenzo's. His wife, Victoria, was expecting their first baby at the end of the year.

Left: The National Aids Trust organised a day conference on 'Women, Aids and the Future', at London's Commonwealth Institute.

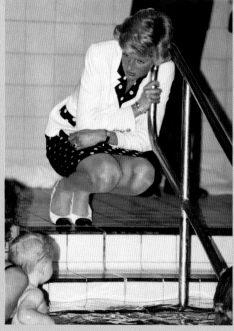

Far left: As part of her work to promote the Health and Fitness campaign 'Swimfit 90', Diana visited the Queen Mother Centre in London.

Left: A visit to Halliwick College, Winchmore Hill in North London, a residential college for students with disabilities.

School sports day

Left: At this year's Wetherby School sports day, Diana came third in the eighty metre mothers' race.

Later in the day, she was seen to smack Prince William, as he ran away when she wanted to leave.

Above: In June, Prince Charles shattered his right arm in a polo accident. It was initially set at a hospital in Cirencester but he had further treatment at the Queen's Medical Centre in Nottingham. A titanium plate was attached to the bone and a piece of bone was taken from his hip to help heal the fracture.

Above left: Resplendent in red and white for the Garter ceremony at Windsor Castle.

Left: Diana greets her sister-in-law, Sarah, at Wimbledon.

Using sign language

Left: At the British Deaf Association centenary congress, she made a faultless speech using sign language. The eight hundred delegates were delighted and gave her a standing ovation. She had been learning to sign for seven years in her role as patron to the association.

Below left: William and Harry arrived at the Queen's Medical Centre to visit their father.

Below right: A very pale-looking Prince Charles leaves the Queen's Medical Centre to travel by helicopter to convalesce at Highgrove. He was still limping and confessed to feeling 'awful'.

Bottom right: Harry's sixth birthday treat was a surprise visit to the Battle of Britain 50th anniversary exhibition with a group of school friends. He had always been interested in the military and here he had the opportunity to sit in the cockpit of a Harrier jump jet and was shown how to operate a World War II Bofors anti-aircraft gun. The group then returned to Kensington Palace for tea.

In September, William began his prep school days at Ludgrove School in Berkshire. The boarding school was reasonably close to Highgrove and Kensington Palace, had a friendly atmosphere and a good sporting reputation. Most significantly, it was set in 130 acres and was set well back from the road, which would give him maximum privacy.

Far left: Diana arrives at the English National Ballet at the Coliseum in London.

Harry's first official function

Left: In October 1990, Harry joined his mother and brother for his first official function. He attended a memorial service at St. Paul's Cathedral for the 1,002 fire fighters who died in the Blitz.

Bottom left: The London Palladium was the venue for a charity gala in October. The celebrity show was held in honour of seven-year-old Lerona Gelb who had been paralysed in a road accident. The show raised £100,000 for the International Spinal Research Trust of which the Princess was patron.

Below: During a day's visit to Portsmouth, Diana played with a rabbit at the Portsea Adventure Playground.

Below left: In October, she made a solo visit on Concorde to Washington DC. There for twenty-two hours, she visited Grandma's House, a home looking after children with Aids, in a very deprived area. She picked up a three-year-old girl, dying of an aids-related illness, who asked for a ride in her car. Diana and her detectives were near to tears after they had given her the treat she so desperately wanted.

Bottom right: A charity gala performance of Noel Coward's *Private Lives* at the Aldwych raised £100,000 for the Royal Marsden Hospital's Cancer Appeal. Joan Collins played one of the lead roles.

Gulf crisis

Left: In November she visited the Gulf Crisis Emergency Unit at the Foreign Office. In the same month, she and Charles returned to Japan for the enthronement of Emperor Akihito.
Below left: On a scheduled visit to Oxford, Diana decided to take an Intercity train from Paddington, accompanied by her bodyguard and lady-in-waiting. After a last minute dash for the train, she too had to endure delays caused by signal failure.
Below: In Colchester, she met Lady Amanda Ellingworth, Trustee of the Guinness Trust.

Charity gala performances

Far left: The London Symphony Orchestra concert at the Barbican was in aid of the Prince's Trust and Birthright.

Left: Glamorous in green, the Princess made a sparkling entrance when she arrived at the The Royal Lancaster Hotel six days later, in early December.

Below: As Diana inspected the graduates at Sandhurst, she sent a message of hope and encouragement to Britain's armed forces. She recognised that many of the cadets would be going straight out to join their regiments in the Gulf.

Below left: The premiere of *Hobson's Choice*.

Compassion and care

Left: At the Children of Eden gala performance at the Prince Edward Theatre, she took time to speak to twelve-year-old Claire Cowdrey.
Below left: During a visit to the FACTS Health co-ordination centre in Crouch End, North London, Diana used every opportunity to talk to patients.
Below: On tour in Peterborough.

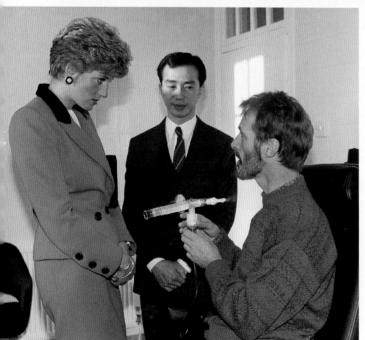

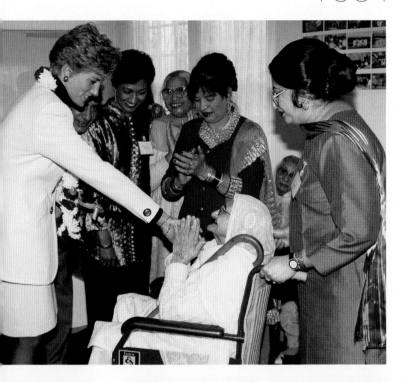

Day out at Alton Towers

Below: Diana loved taking William and Harry to 'ordinary' places so they could enjoy days out like any other family. Accompanied only by bodyguards, they queued up for rides and she insisted that they were given no special privileges. The boys had a wonderful time.

Left: In her capacity as patron of Help the Aged, Diana visited three hundred old people at an Asian Centre in Southall.

Below left: The unveiling of the commemorative plaque when Diana opened the Oxford and Bedford Houses at Broadmoor Hospital.

Easter visits

Left: The royal premiere of *LA Story* was held at the Canon cinema in Shaftesbury Avenue.

Bottom: During a visit to Great Ormond Street Hospital, the Princess stopped to talk to the mother of David Meaney, a three-year-old boy suffering from brain damage. During the conversation, Diana quietly stroked the boy's hand and he woke for a moment.

Below: At Windsor, with the Royal Family, for the Easter Service.

The school run

Left: Whenever possible, Diana would try to drop the boys at school herself. On this chilly morning, she had just taken William to Wetherby School after the Easter break.

Below: A dinner was held at the Mansion House to mark the launch of the Re Action Trust, a charitable venture between industry and Help the Aged. During her speech, Diana urged people to consider how much older people can still contribute to society.

Royal visit to Brazil

Left: In April the Prince and Princess visited Brazil. During their stay, Diana took advantage of the hotel pool to have a very brief morning dip.

Above left: Matching outfits for the Prince and Princess. They still maintained a happy image of their marriage when at official functions.

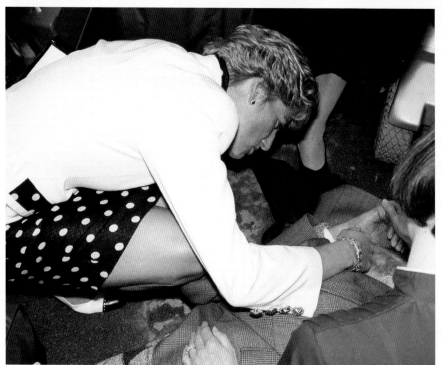

Helping others at home and abroad

Above left: The Simple Truth charity concert at Wembley Arena raised £10 million pounds to help the Kurdish refugees. Within hours of the concert finishing, money was to be sent to northern Iraq and would be closely followed by food, blankets and medical supplies. The money raised was to be matched by £10 million pledged by the government. Diana arrived at Wembley to support the cause.

Left and above: During a visit to open a new day hospital and family health clinic at Marlow Community Hospital in Buckinghamshire, the Princess went on a walkabout outside to meet the waiting crowds. When one elderly gentleman collapsed, she made her way through the crowds to kneel down and comfort him until the ambulance arrived.

Royal curtsey

Left: Protocol demanded that she curtsey to the Queen at a Mansion House function. In June, William, while at school, was accidentally hit with a golf club by a friend, knocking him unconscious. With blood pouring from the wound, he was rushed to the Royal Berkshire Hospital. His parents disagreed over which hospital should treat him but in the end Diana had her wish and he was sent to Great Ormond Street Hospital for Sick Children under police escort. He had a depressed fracture of the skull and needed a seventy-five minute operation to assess the damage that had been caused. Diana stayed with him while Charles had to continue with his royal duties. William eventually made a full recovery.

Above left: Diana met Elton John during a charity performance of *Tango Argentino* at the Aldwych Theatre. Proceeds went to the National Aids Trust.

Above: With Harry now at Wetherby, it was soon time for Diana to enter the annual Mothers' race once again.

Thirtieth birthday

Above: In early July, the Prince and Princess were at the Royal Albert Hall for a gala performance of Verdi's *Requiem* by the London Symphony Chorus. It had been the Princess's thirtieth birthday a week earlier and press reports claimed that Charles had offered to throw a party for her at Highgrove but that she had declined. On the day she attended a lunch party at the Savoy in aid of the Rainbow House children's hospice appeal.

Above left: Always a keen tennis fan, Diana was at Wimbledon.

Left: After the premiere of *Backdraft* at the Empire, Leicester Square, introductions were made to Kurt Russell and William Baldwin.

Summer holidays over

Left: After the annual summer break at Balmoral, Diana and the boys flew back with Prince Andrew and his daughters. There was time for a quick peck before the two families left in separate cars.
Below left: As colonel-in-chief of the Royal Hampshire regiment, she attended the regimental parade.
Below: A gentle touch for one of the patients at the Royal Hospital and Home, Putney. The centre treated severely disabled people.

Celebration and tears

Left: His Aunt Sarah and cousins, Eugenie and Beatrice, joined in Harry's seventh birthday celebrations. A special birthday surprise was laid on in the grounds of Kensington Palace, which included a display by the police dog-handling team. Other people in the park watched as Harry whooped with delight at the sight of the dog-handler team clowning around with a display of cops and robber chases in which the dogs broke up fights between policemen wielding baseball bats.

Below: In October, Diana was on an official engagement in the Midlands, when news reached her that five-year-old Leonora Knatchbull had died after a fourteen-month fight against cancer. She was the great-granddaughter of Lord Mountbatten and her parents, Lord and Lady Romsey, were very close friends of the Prince and Princess of Wales. Only a few days earlier, Diana had spent several hours at the hospital with Leonora.

Below left: In September, Diana made a solo four-day tour of Pakistan. She visited a Family Welfare Centre in a small village just outside Islamabad, receiving a traditional garland when she arrived.

Canadian tour

Left: In October, the whole family were involved in the official tour of Canada. The boys flew out the day before their parents, for security reasons. The tour marked the start of William's grooming for his future role and he was to accompany his parents on some occasions, in an official capacity.

Top: One of the Princess's favourite photographs, which she kept in her dressing room in Kensington Palace. She had just flown into Toronto and had to endure a marathon reception before she could see her children. She rushed across the deck of the Royal Yacht *Britannia* and threw her arms round them.

Above: Aboard a helicopter as it flew over Niagara Falls.

Further work with the National Aids Trust

Below and bottom: At a conference organised by the National Aids Trust, Diana listened to teenagers' views on ways to improve sex education, to help protect young people from contracting the HIV virus. She listened carefully to their ideas, often making notes, and met them more informally afterwards.
Left: At Milestone House, Diana had tea with a lady suffering from Aids.

Dance for Life

The Dance for Life event at Her Majesty's Theatre marked World Aids Day. The evening featured the Royal Ballet and dancers from *Cats* and *Phantom of the Opera*, raising £150,000 for Crusaid. It was only three months since Diana's close friend Adrian Ward-Jackson, Governor of the Royal Ballet, had died of an Aids-related illness.

Above left: When presenting the Princess with flowers, four-year-old Nicola Gerry asked Diana for a kiss.

Left: Meeting ballet dancer Darcey Bussell, after the show.

Above: Seven-year-old Harry holds his mother's hand on the way to Sandringham on Christmas Day.

In 1991, *Hello!* magazine voted Diana 'the most elegant and stylish woman of the year'.

Tour of India

Left: At the Taj Mahal, on a visit to India, Diana spent several minutes in solitude. The Taj had been erected by Moghul Emperor Shah Jahan, as a memorial to his wife, who died in childbirth. This was the photograph, published around the world, that seemed to confirm Diana's loneliness and unhappiness in her marriage.

Below: In a very moving visit, Diana met many disabled 'untouchables', also known as 'God's People', who were from the lowest Indian castes. They gave her the traditional sign of respect by reaching for her ankles and she immediately moved closer and spoke to them through an interpreter. She met them at a welfare centre where residents were supported by British donors in an 'adopt a granny' scheme. It was run by Help the Aged - the Princess being a patron – who were supporting 6,000 elderly people in India at the time. After Charles had left at the end of the tour, Diana visited Mother Teresa's hospice in Calcutta, meeting every patient who was near to death.

Below left: The Prince and Princess during the tour.

1992

Meeting Mother Teresa

Left: Soon after the India tour, Diana travelled to Rome where she had the opportunity to meet Mother Teresa.

Bottom left: When Diana presented medals after a polo match, the 20,000 strong crowd watched as Prince Charles moved to kiss his wife. However, Diana deliberately turned at the last moment to avoid his embrace.

Below left: A visit to the Institute of Child Health.

Below right: The royal premiere of *Hear My Song* raised £75,000 for Turning Point. The Princess addressed the audience, asking them to try to understand the plight of the mentally ill. During the evening, Josef Locke, on whose life the film was based, became one of Michael Aspel's victims for *This Is Your Life*. The Princess had known about the plan and delightedly joined in with the applause.

Bottom right: In her role as President of Barnardo's, she made a visit to the St. Luke's Day Care Centre in Deptford.

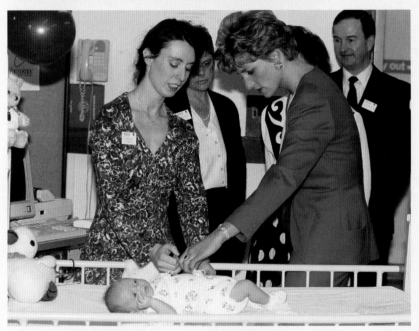

The death of Earl Spencer

Above left and above: In March, Diana's father, Earl Spencer, died from a heart attack at the age of sixty-eight. Diana adored her father, who had passed away while she was on a skiing holiday. The funeral at the church of St. Mary the Virgin, near the Althorp Estate in Northamptonshire, included many joyful hymns at the Earl's express wish. Diana's message of farewell on a wreath of lilies, sweet peas, stocks and freesias said simply, 'I will miss you dreadfully, darling daddy, but will love you forever. Love Diana.' The service helped to reunite the Earl's three daughters with their stepmother, Raine.

Left: In May, friends and family gathered at St. Margaret's Westminster to pay tribute to the late Earl Spencer, in a moving memorial service. The Rev. Dr. Donald Grey, Canon of Westminster, led the service. He summed up the Earl as 'a loyal husband, a loving father and a uniquely wonderful grandparent'. Bank of England Governor Robin Leigh-Pemberton, who had known the Earl since their schooldays, gave the address.

Solo tour of Egypt

Left: On a solo trip to Egypt, Diana visited the pyramids. Apparently, photographers were very disappointed with the colour of her outfit, as it blended into the background.

Above left: Britain's leading acappella group, 'Black Voices', was invited to perform at St. Stephen Walbrook, a church in the City of London. Diana thoroughly enjoyed the performance and met the singers afterwards.

Above: With her boys, after the Easter Service at Windsor.

Distress at drug addiction

Left: Diana was asked to make a keynote speech at a Turning Point conference. However, after watching the premiere of a ten-minute film on drug addiction, she was visibly distressed and needed time to compose herself before speaking to the audience.

Below left and below: The Prince and Princess arrived separately for the Garter Ceremony at Windsor Castle when Sir Edward Heath, Viscount Ridley and Baron Sainsbury were installed as Knights of the Garter. Although they smiled and waved to the crowds there was very little communication between them.

In June, the Andrew Morton book, *Diana, Her True Story,* was published, which claimed to tell the truth about Diana's unhappiness. He had used material from interviews with Diana's friends. There was much speculation about Diana's involvement in the content and detail of the book. After this, Charles and Diana were barely on speaking terms.

Visits around Britain

Above left: A visit to the Erskine Hospital for Disabled Servicemen in Glasgow.

Above: Despite the obvious security risks, the Princess delighted the people of Belfast by visiting the newly restored Church House headquarters of the Presbyterian Church in Ireland and later attended a garden party at Hillsborough Castle.

Below: With the children at a Barnardo's conference.

Left: A bouquet from two-year-old Jade Symons at the Royal Albert Hall.

The Proms

Above: Crowds gather to welcome Diana to the First Night of the Proms at the Royal Albert Hall.
Above left: A perfectly co-ordinated Princess at the opening night of the Australian ballet at the London Coliseum.
Left: At the First Night of the Proms she was greeted by Prime Minister John Major.

Greek island tour

Left: In August, Charles and Diana took their sons to Greece to begin a cruise in the Ionian Sea. They boarded a luxury cruise ship, the *Alexander*, lent to them by family friend and oil tycoon, John Latsis. The ship was equipped with three speedboats, an eight-seater helicopter and a chandeliered ballroom. The holiday was widely seen to be a last attempt to repair their ailing marriage.

Below: Meeting a patient at the London Lighthouse hospice.

Below left: Diana dazzled the crowds when she arrived for the royal charity premiere of *Just Like A Woman*. The evening raised vital funds for leukaemia research and she later met the film's star, Julie Walters, whose daughter Maisie suffered from the illness.

Bottom: The Prince and Princess arrived together for the commemoration service marking the 50th anniversary of the battle of El Alamein.

Half-term treat

Above: At Earls Court for the Queen's 40th Anniversary Gala.
Right: The Princess won praise from Junior Health Minister Baroness Cumberledge who, at an Aids conference, credited Diana with having a significant influence on government policy.
Below: For an October half-term treat, Diana took the boys to Buckmore Park near Rochester in Kent. She had bought go-karts for them and they confidently raced the machines around the track at speeds of up to 50mph.

Royal visit to South Korea

Above left: On a four-day visit to South Korea, Diana visited the Seoul British School.

Above: Honouring troops at the Welsh Guards Memorial Service.

Left: Addressing drug abuse specialists.

Below left: Diana was only too delighted to meet Paul and Linda McCartney when he performed his Oratorio at a concert hall in Lille.

Below: Diana meets Wayne Sleep again after a charity performance of the Nutcracker by the English National Ballet. The event, hosted by Foreign Secretary Douglas Hurd, raised money for English National Ballet and the Foundation for Conductive Education, which was aiming to build a national institution, mainly for the treatment of children suffering from cerebral palsy.

The marriage ends

Opposite: The royal couple were clearly unhappy in each other's company.

Above: The Royal Variety Performance was the last joint engagement before their separation. On 9th December, it was announced in the House of Commons, by Prime Minister, John Major, that the Prince and Princess of Wales were to part. There was to be no question of divorce, and if Charles were to become King, she would become Queen. The previous week, they had both removed belongings from their respective homes – Charles would now officially be at Highgrove and Diana at Kensington Palace.

Left: Diana left Buckingham Palace, alone, after the announcement.

High jinks at Thorpe Park

With only their nanny and personal detectives in tow, Diana took William and Harry to Thorpe Park, their favourite theme park. Dressed in jeans and sweatshirts, they queued up and enjoyed the thrills of the rides, often getting soaked in spray!

The Jungle Book

Left: Diana joined families all over Britain by taking her sons to see *The Jungle Book*. The twenty-six-year old film had been re-released for the third time, with more than five million people buying tickets to net in excess of £4 million.

Below left: In a very moving speech, Diana spoke to a large audience of health professionals at the Eating Disorders conference. She spoke of the despair and lack of self-esteem people endured and obviously drew on memories from her early childhood. Diana was believed to have suffered from bulimia during the early years of her marriage.

Below: A dinner for the British Wheelchair Sports Foundation at the Banqueting House, London.

Colonel-in-chief

Left: In June, Diana attended a military ceremony to take up the post of colonel-in-chief to the newly formed Princess of Wales's Royal Regiment. It had been created from a merger of the Queen's and the Royal Hampshires and troops had already been nicknamed 'Di's Guys'. She watched as a team of free-fall parachutists dropped from 3,000 feet to present her with a gold and diamond regimental brooch. During the ceremony, Diana addressed the troops, and to the delight of the crowd announced, 'It has to be said that for a thirty-one-year-old woman to have 2,500 men under her command is quite a feat, but I am sure I will rise to the occasion'!

Below: On walkabout in Cambridge town centre.

Below left: On walkabout in Oxford.

Bottom left: Diana meets opera singer, Rebecca Evans.

Bottom: Supporting the Serpentine Gallery Renovation Appeal.

Visiting the sick and needy in Zimbabwe

Above: A visit to Zimbabwe soon became known as 'the suffering tour' as she met and comforted the sick, those dying from Aids related illnesses and leprosy victims. She flew out to see the work being done by the major charities, who were delighted to involve her; Diana's presence was guaranteed to highlight any cause quickly and effectively. She was also highly respected for her genuine compassion and concern.

Above left: Diana was greeted by the Brazilian ambassador, Senor Paulo-Tarso Flecha-Lima at Tiffany's in Bond Street, where she viewed the Schlumberger jewellery collection. His wife Lucia was a very close friend of Diana's, giving the Princess a great deal of support when she needed it most.

Left: Diana spoke to children on a very successful tour of Nepal. She travelled with Lynda Chalker, Minister for Overseas Development, visiting British Aid projects. During the year, it had became clear that Diana's official foreign trips would become more limited but she was determined to continue the charity work that she knew was so effective. She therefore approached charities such as the International Red Cross, who were delighted to work with her in organising future foreign visits.

Death of Lady Ruth Fermoy

Left: The Prince and Princess were briefly reunited at the funeral of Diana's maternal grandmother, Lady Ruth Fermoy, when they arrived together for the service at St. Margaret's Church in King's Lynn. They accompanied the Queen Mother, who had lost her oldest and closest friend and also her lady-in-waiting for three decades. Lady Fermoy had found her loyalties divided when Charles and Diana's marriage broke down, but despite reports of a rift between Diana and her grandmother, they had spent a great deal of time together just before she died. After the internment at St. Mary Magdalen's, Sandringham, the Prince and Princess left in separate helicopters.

Above left and above: At the Red Cross feeding station at Mazerera, Diana took on the role of feeding the children, some of whom had to walk ten miles a day to reach the centre. She dished out the meal of dhovi – a stew of ground peanuts, French beans, cooking oil and refined meal. The children were delighted when she gave out double the normal rations.

A separate Christmas

Left: On Christmas Day, Diana was resplendent in scarlet and black as she walked to church for the Christmas Day service. However, afterwards, she kissed William and Harry and spent Christmas elsewhere.

Above left: A relaxed and tanned Diana watching the performance at the Indiana Jones Adventure, Walt Disney World, Florida. She had taken the boys there in August.

Above: As Diana performed her penultimate public engagement, she opened the St. Matthew's Community Centre at the Elephant and Castle in South London. Her hand was kissed by a loyal fan! On 3rd December, during a function at the Hilton hotel, Diana decided to step down from public life. She stated that she needed 'time and space' after being the centre of media attention for twelve years.

Reunion with Mother Teresa

Above left: Diana met Mother Teresa at the Missionaries of Charity in Kilburn and the two greeted each other like old friends. Mother Teresa had flown into England en route from Washington to India, especially to see Diana. The two women had a great deal of respect for each other's work and Diana was invited to return to Calcutta to see the progress the mission had made on the streets.

Above: At a family lunch at Scalini's, Diana met up with her brother, Earl Spencer, and her mother, Frances Shand Kydd. Charles Spencer's wife, Victoria, and their eldest daughter Kitty, aged three, accompanied them. They also had twin girls, Eliza and Amelia, aged seventeen months and Victoria was pregnant with their fourth child, due the following month.

Left: Diana travelled from Paddington, with four friends, to watch the Wales v France international at Cardiff Arms Park. She clearly enjoyed herself amongst old friends, who produced a picnic lunch and bottles of Pouilly-Fumé!

Heir to the Althorp Estate

Above left: Earl Spencer's wife, Victoria, gave birth to a boy, Louis Frederick in April. As their first son, he would inherit the title Viscount Althorp and the £90 million family estate. Diana arrived at St. Mary's, Paddington, to visit her new nephew. She came without any security protection and had to make her way through waiting photographers to get into the hospital.

Above: Diana joined William van Straubenzee, Catherine Soames and Kate Manzies for lunch at San Lorenzo's. Unable to park nearby, she had asked two Metropolitan Police officers to protect her car from traffic wardens, so they put official memos under the windscreen wipers.

Left: Diana later found out that the two officers had been pulled up for their actions and was fully intent on apologising to them.

Camilla Parker Bowles

On 29th June, a documentary about Prince Charles, produced by Jonathan Dimbleby, was broadcast on television. During the interview, Charles admitted to adultery, after his marriage to Diana had broken down. The next day, Camilla Parker Bowles was named. He had had a relationship with her before she married her husband Andrew, and they had always remained very close friends. The night the programme went out to an audience of fourteen million, Diana attended a *Vanity Fair* party at the Serpentine Gallery. She wore a headline-grabbing black cocktail dress (*right*).

Below and bottom: Diana arrived with Prince William to watch the women's final at Wimbledon. She sat with the Duchess of Kent.

Shopping in London
Diana had always enjoyed shopping in Kensington High Street and could now move around more freely without having to be accompanied by protection officers.

Official visit to Paris

Right: In her capacity as President of Barnardo's, Diana made her first official overseas visit since she withdrew from public life the previous year. She had an informal lunch with President Valery Giscard d'Estaing and his wife, to foster links between Barnardo's and its French equivalent. From this moment onwards, she was to gradually resume more official and charity work.

Above: Guest of honour at a Versailles society ball in aid of a French children's charity.

Below: Diana arrived at the Headway National Head Injuries Association fund-raising Christmas lunch.

Below right: Surrounded by admirers.

Christmas
Above: Christmas Day with William and Harry.

Raising the alarm

Left: In January, Diana arrived at the Royal Parks Office in Hyde Park to present Royal Humane Society Awards to two men who had rescued a drowning tramp from a lake in Regent's Park. The Princess had been jogging in the park and had been the first person to raise the alarm. This was her first official engagement since the announcement of Camilla Parker Bowles's divorce at the beginning of the year.

Above: Diana took William and a school friend to Cardiff Arms Park to watch Ireland beat Wales 16-12.

Below: Diana at London Fashion Week.

Visit to Japan

Right and below: On a visit to Japan, she delighted her hosts by speaking to them briefly in Japanese, one of the most difficult languages to master. She had been coached at Kensington Palace for the past year. She then went on to give a message of compassion for the victims of the Kobe earthquake. At the Tokyo children's hospital, one little girl thought she was Cinderella.

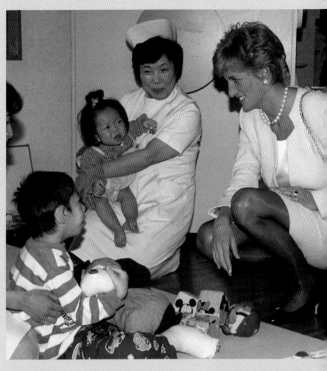

Di's Guys

Right: The Princess returned to Canterbury to inspect the Princess of Wales's Royal Regiment at Howe Barracks. She was there to hand over the new colours to the regiment and was wearing the brooch presented to her by the free-fall parachute team on her previous visit.

Above: While there, Diana met World War I veteran Bill Pierce, who was one hundred and four years old.

Russia and Venice

It was now two-and-a-half years since Diana's separation from Prince Charles and her public appearances, such as trips to Moscow and Venice, were becoming rare. At thirty three, the figure of the world's most photographed woman was changing too. In recent months she had been pursuing a rigorous training schedule in the gym and there was now a new outline to her once slim shoulders.

Above: Diana was patron of a trust fund set up to improve facilities at the Tushinskaya Children's Hospital in Moscow. The hospital was struggling to care for more than a thousand children and while there she met nurses at the training school.

Left and Below: Diana in Venice with one of her new friends Hong Kong-Chinese millionaire and fellow art lover, David Tang.

Unsung work with the homeless

Left and below: In June, Diana opened a hostel in
Willesden, North London, run by the Depaul Trust.
During the day, Cardinal Basil Hume paid tribute to
Diana's work with the homeless; he revealed that she
would often make private visits to hostels.
Above: Choosing a Versace dress, the Princess met
Tom Hanks at the premiere of *Apollo 13*.
In July, the family took part in their last official
engagement together. They attended the 50th
anniversary celebrations of VJ Day in London and
had appeared to be very happy as they sat watching
the parade.

William's first day at Eton

Left: William successfully passed his Common Entrance Examination and arrived for his first day at Eton in September 1995. Despite the fact that his parents were in the midst of divorce proceedings, the whole family arrived together. Diana had always wanted her boys to attend the school, following in the footsteps of the Spencer family.

Below left, below, and bottom: Diana was invited to Argentina by the ALPI medical charity. While there, she met the Argentinian president, toured hospitals and met juveniles drawn into drink and drugs rings. During a lighter moment, she watched the whales in Puerto Piamides. On 20th November, Diana took part in a *Panorama* interview with reporter Martin Bashir. The programme captured an audience of twenty-three million as Diana talked about her eating disorders and admitted to a relationship with James Hewitt, who had since let her down. She openly discussed her relationship with Charles, which could not work as 'there were three of us in this marriage'.

Humanitarian of the Year
In a glittering ceremony in New York, Diana shared the award of Humanitarian of the Year with General Colin Powell(*left*). The award, presented at New York's Hilton Hotel, marked her caring and compassionate achievements over the past fifteen years. She made her acceptance speech to guests who had paid £750 a head to attend.

Media attention

Above and above right: Diana in Kensington High Street. At times she could shop almost anonymously; at other times, photographers would surround her. She was now able to move about without an official protection team and although it gave her more freedom, it had its downsides; she was often frustrated and upset by the continual attention of the media.

Left: Diana took Chicago by storm when she arrived in June. Everywhere she went, crowds cheered and emotions ran high. One young boy reached out from the crowd to embrace her. She was there to raise money for breast cancer treatment, and attended the symposium on breast cancer at Northwestern University in Chicago.

Decree absolute

Above and left: The divorce settlement was finally agreed between Charles and Diana, with the decree nisi announced on 15th July. Six weeks later when it was followed by the decree absolute, Diana fulfilled a previously planned commitment to visit the English National Ballet. She was still wearing her wedding and engagement rings. Charles was five hundred miles away at Balmoral, with William and Harry.

Above left: At a gala dinner in Chicago, Diana danced with American chat-show host Phil Donahue, amongst the dinosaurs at the Natural History Museum!

Divorce agreement

Under the terms of the divorce, Diana received a lump sum payment in the region of £17 million, but the title 'Her Royal Highness' was taken away. She decided to withdraw her support from a hundred charities, only maintaining involvement with six favourites: the National Aids Trust; the Leprosy Mission; Victor Adebowale's Centrepoint; the Royal Marsden NHS Trust; the English National Ballet; and the Great Ormond Street Hospital. She was trying to reduce her workload and concentrate on her future life as a single woman.

Left and below: Official functions in London.

Above: In October Diana flew to Rimini, where she was presented with a humanitarian award for drawing attention to the under-privileged.

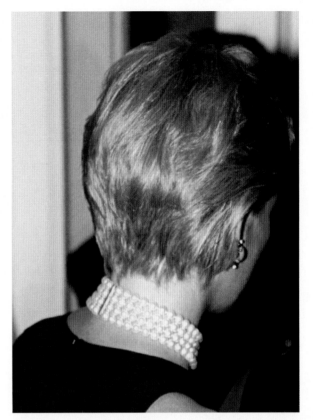

A discreet love affair

Top left: Sitting with heart surgeon Christian Barnard at the award dinner in Rimini. At the time, there was media speculation about a romance between Diana and heart surgeon Dr. Hasnat Khan, whom she met in 1995 while visiting a friend at the Royal Brompton Hospital. The relationship was serious, the Princess even visiting his family in Pakistan in 1996 while she was there seeing her friend Jemima Khan, but the couple worked hard to keep out of the limelight. The relationship between Khan and the Princess, which ended shortly before her death, was the subject of the 2013 film *Diana* starring Naomi Watts.

Top right: Sporting a new, sleeker hairstyle.

Above: At the end of the year Diana took Prince Harry, now aged twelve, to a performance of *Riverdance*.

Right: With Mohamed Al Fayed for the launch of the *Heart of Britain* book at Harrods.

Campaign against landmines

It was the Red Cross that first brought the landmine issue to Diana's attention. After watching a film premiere in aid of the charity, which was trying to instigate a world-wide ban on the weapon, Diana realised that this was another major issue where she could make a difference. A publicity visit to Angola was organised in January, with Diana travelling on behalf of the Red Cross.

Walking through a minefield

Diana was escorted by Mike Whitlam, director general of the charity in Britain. On arrival in Luanda they attended a mines awareness briefing session, where it was revealed that there was one amputee for every 384 inhabitants. She visited the most heavily mined areas and toured hospitals where she spoke to adults and children injured by stepping on mines. Shocked by what she had seen, she was determined to bring this issue to the world's attention. Working with the Halo Trust, the mine clearance team, she walked through the middle of a half-cleared minefield, knowing the global impact the photograph would have. *Below:* On departure from Angola.

William's confirmation

Left: Prince William was confirmed in March 1997 at St. George's Chapel, Windsor. It was the first time that Charles and Diana had been seen together in public since their divorce the previous August. By this time, Charles and Diana's relationship had improved and they seemed more comfortable in each other's company. He would drop in to see her at Kensington Palace and they would attend the children's school events together.

Last hospital visits

Above right: In April, Diana visited cystic fibrosis sufferers at the Royal Brompton Hospital in London.

In June, she flew to Washington to help launch the American Red Cross anti-landmines campaign, attending a gala evening that raised $650,000 for the charity. Moving on to New York, she met with Mother Teresa and attended a breakfast meeting with Hillary Clinton. At the end of the month there was a charity sale of her dresses – an idea sparked by Prince William. Eight hundred guests paid over £100 each to attend the preview party and the final sale raised over $3 million, with most of the proceeds going to the Aids Crisis Trust.

Above and right: A new children's wing was opened at Northwick Park Hospital on 21st July.

Continuing the campaign in Bosnia

In August, Diana flew out for a four-day visit to Bosnia, continuing to promote the Red Cross landmines campaign. She met landmine victims and bereaved relatives of those killed by the blasts, often reduced to tears by their plight.

Prior to the visit, she had been holidaying with William and Harry in St. Tropez where they were the guests of Mohamed Al Fayed, on his luxury yacht. While there she met his son Dodi and there was much speculation in the media about a possible romance. On her return from Bosnia, she spent some time with her friend Rosa Monckton, cruising around the Greek islands, before returning to France with Dodi on 21st August. She had left England for the last time.

Death of a Princess

On Saturday 30th August, Diana and Dodi were in Paris and went to the Ritz for dinner. When they left, they were besieged by the paparazzi and the Mercedes, in which they were travelling at high speed, crashed in a tunnel running parallel to the Seine.

Dodi was killed instantly, while Diana was cut free and rushed to a Paris hospital. However, after two massive heart attacks Diana could not be resuscitated and died in the early hours of Sunday morning.

Her sons were at Balmoral with Prince Charles and he had the daunting task of telling them the news when they woke that morning. He then flew out to Paris to escort her body back to England. People around the world were stunned by the news and messages of sympathy poured in. At Kensington Palace, the sea of floral tributes grew by the minute and people queued for hours to sign books of condolences.

The *Mail* 85p
ON SUNDAY
AUGUST 31, 1997

Appalling tragedy shocks the world

DIANA DIES AFTER PARIS CAR CRASH

THE CARING PRINCESS – NO LONGER WITH US

Mail on Sunday Reporters

DIANA, Princess of Wales was killed early today. She died in a Paris hospital hours after a horrific car crash in which her boyfriend Dodi Fayed was also killed.
The tragedy which stunned Britain and the world came during a high-speed chase through the city with
Continued on Page 2

Last farewell

Diana's funeral took place in Westminster Abbey on Saturday 6th September, with an estimated one million people pouring into London to line the procession route. In silence, they paid their last respects as the funeral cortège moved past, with her sons, Prince Charles, her brother Earl Spencer and Prince Philip keeping pace behind the coffin. After the dignified and moving service, thousands more lined the streets as the hearse took her body on its final journey to the Spencer estate at Althorp, where she was to be laid to rest on an island during a private family burial.

Above: An aerial view of the island on the Althorp Estate, Northamptonshire, where Diana's body was laid to rest.

Sentabale – Forget-me-Not

Left: The Princes attended the unveiling of the Diana Memorial Fountain in Hyde Park on 6 July 2004.

Middle Left: In April 2006 Harry was reunited with six-year-old Mutsu Potsane in the grounds of the Mants'ase Children's Home in Lesotho. The Prince was there to launch his charity Sentebale, the Princes' Fund for Lesotho. Formed jointly with Prince Seeiso, the charity aims to help children who have been orphaned by Aids. The name Sentebale means 'Forget-me-not' and was chosen in memory of both the Princes' mothers. Stating that inspiration had come from his mother's dedication to her work, Prince Harry plans to commit himself to this charity for life.

Bottom left: In 2008 the Princes travelled to South Africa and helped raise money for Unicef, the Nelson Mandela Children's Fund and Sentebale.

Below: Princes William and Harry helped the Tsunami Appeal when they spent a day working with the Red Cross packing hygiene kits to send out to the Maldives. Both were there at their own request, having seen the news coverage. The Princes have followed in their mother's footsteps by committing themselves to charity work. While Harry has spent time in Africa, William has focused his attention on the homeless. In September 2005, he became the Patron of Centrepoint, the main UK charity working with homeless youths. He has made frequent visits to various charities for the homeless, and began his patronage of Centrepoint by spending several days talking to the young people there and helping them with their immediate needs.

Bottom right: Harry, referred to as Lieutenant Henry Wales, receives his provisional wings from his father.

A new generation

Left: Clarence House announced the engagement of Prince William and Kate Middleton on 16 November 2010. William gave her the sapphire and diamond engagement ring that had belonged to his mother.

Below: On 23 July 2013 Kate and William presented their baby son to the assembled press corps in a scene reminiscent of that in June 1982 when Charles and Diana stood on the steps of the Lindo Wing in Paddington holding the newly born Prince William.

First published in 2011
This revised and updated edition published by Atlantic World in 2013

Atlantic World
38 Copthorne Road
Croxley Green
WD3 4 AQ
United Kingdom

All images © Associated Newspapers
Text by Alison Gauntlett
This collection © Atlantic Publishing 2013

A catalogue record for this book is available
from the British Library.

Hardback ISBN: 978-1-909242-47-0
Paperback ISBN: 978-1-909242-40-1

Printed in China